The Corporate Christian

Christian Beliefs vs. Corporate Behaviors

Pastor Owen E. Williams

Order this book online at www.trafford.com
or email orders@trafford.com

Most Trafford titles are also available at major online book retailers.

© Copyright 2012 Pastor Owen E. Williams.
All rights reserved. No part of this publication may be reproduced, stored in a retrieval system, or transmitted, in any form or by any means, electronic, mechanical, photocopying, recording, or otherwise, without the written prior permission of the author.

John Mac Arthur Study bible allows up 1,000 verses to be quoted as long as they don't add up to over 50% of the complete book

Contact Pastor Williams at OEWilliamsMinistries.com

Printed in the United States of America.

ISBN: 978-1-4669-2047-7 (sc)
ISBN: 978-1-4669-2046-0 (hc)
ISBN: 978-1-4669-2048-4 (e)

Library of Congress Control Number: 2012904916

Trafford rev. 04/13/2012

 www.trafford.com

North America & international
toll-free: 1 888 232 4444 (USA & Canada)
phone: 250 383 6864 ♦ fax: 812 355 4082

Dedication

Thank you to my wife of twenty-one years, Elder Debora Williams, for her continued support in this project. Thank you for your valuable input from your twenty-seven years of experience in corporate America. Thank you for your consistent study of God's Word and collaboration. Thank you for your typing, typing, and retyping of this labor of love.

Thank you to my daughter, the love and joy of my life, my one and only Desiree Rose, who is the fuel that keeps me going.

Endorsements

Dr. Linda C. Lombardi

Dr. Linda C. Lombardi has been an Adjunct Professor at New York University for two decades:

There are all sorts of travel books, some allow the reader to see foreign lands, others search for adventures in deep forests and then there are ones like The Corporate Christian. This book takes the reader on a journey inward, a soul-searching exploration of the modern world and ethics. Filled with insights and raw experience . . . the perfect book for the seeker in all of us. In this age of change, Pastor Williams' insights, a guidebook, that provides clarity, direction and hope. A must-read for those who struggle to balance the demands of corporate life.

> N. J. L'Heureux
> Executive Director
> Queens Federation of Churches

Rev N.J.L' Heureux has been the Executive Director Queens Ferderation of Churches for over thirty-five years:

Pastor Owen Williams puts his finger and pen on a serious issue confronting Christians who wish to live and behave ethically when confronted with a corporate culture that is all-to-often willing to prefer profits to people. He acknowledges that this is hard work, making daily choices to bring integrity to the workplace and wholeness to life. God created us for his own purposes and not for the purpose of serving corporate-interests. We have to acknowledge that the only legitimate basis for a corporation is to serve the needs of people. The language of "customer care" becomes meaningful only as corporate leaders bring the values of their faith into their offices.

Contents

Preface xiii

Acknowledgments xv

Introduction: A Standard of Confusion xvii

Chapter 1 1
The Promoted Corporate Culture
- Diversity
- Human Development
- Training

Chapter 2 9
The Unpromoted Subculture
- Politics
- Favoritism
- Cronyism
- Corruption
- Destruction of Ethics and Innocence

Chapter 3 15
The Christian Faith
- The Panoptic Message of the Gospels
- The Philosophy of the Gospel
- The Practicality of the Gospel
- The Purity of the Gospel

Chapter 4 .... **23**
A Corporation
- Definition and Structure
- The Goal
- The Philosophy
- The Practicality

Chapter 5 .... **29**
The Continental Divide
- The Motivation of the Message
- The Gospel Message
- The Believer versus the Employee
- The Rewards and Benefits

Chapter 6 .... **41**
The Coexistence
- The Covenant
- The Responsibilities of Both
- Stewardship or Ownership

Chapter 7 .... **49**
Reconciliation of Christianity and Corporation Christians
- The Spirit of God
- The Corporate Christian's Walk
- Reasons Why Reconciliation Is Never Done

Chapter 8 .... **59**
Stress Factors
- Stress and the Corporate Environment
- Stress and the Body, Physically and Emotionally
- The Foundation of Stress

Chapter 9 65
Dysfunctional Behavior
- Abnormal Behavior
- Psychological Reasons

Chapter 10 71
Disunity
- Dissenting Behavior
- Reasons for Dissenting Behavior
- God's Principle of Unity

Chapter 11 79
Disorderly Conduct
- Decency and Order
- Responsibility for Order
- Diffusion of Responsibility

Chapter 12 85
Rising Out of the Ashes, a Bright Future
- Now That We're Here
- A Legacy of Integrity
- The Power of Difference

Preface

This book was birthed out of a strong desire to encourage the hundreds of thousands of men and women who have the unique, rewarding, and even heartbreaking assignments serving our Lord and Savior as corporate Christians.

Its aim is to capture the intangible struggles of the emotions, hearts, and minds of this audience who on a daily basis must fight to reconcile their beliefs with their behavior so they agree with each other.

The corporate Christian is that man or woman who has, by God's grace and favor, advanced to positions of influence in the corporate environment while desperately trying not to compromise the fundamental principles of the faith.

In the upcoming chapters, we will attempt to identify a few of the struggles, trials, pitfalls, and hard daily decisions these individuals must make as they serve two masters.

Acknowledgments

I would like to take this opportunity to thank the following people, for without their contributions, this book would not be possible.

To my Lord and Savior Jesus Christ, who looks past my sins and faults and continues to bestow His everlasting power, grace, and mercy upon me.

To my beloved wife and partner for life, Elder Debora Williams, for her continued love, support, and encouragement toward me, even when it's not deserved. To my beautiful daughter, Desiree Williams, for the glorious privilege of watching her grow up into the exceptional young woman she is today.

To my mother, Beverly Williams, who taught me to give until it hurts.

Acknowledgments

To my father, O. E. Williams, who taught me discipline and structure.

To my spiritual father in the gospel, Bishop Charles E. Betts Sr., who prays for me and patiently helped me develop in the pastoral ministry.

To my spiritual stepfather, Pastor Crawford Hinson, and the Friendship Baptist Church congregation for their endless love, prayers, and support.

To Pastors John and Fanny Walker, who demonstrated their trust and faith in me by turning over their life's work into my hands.

To my St. Mark family for the care, concern, love, prayers, and support they have always shown to me, my wife, and my entire family.

To my beloved aunt Myrtle English, who has always shown love and compassion and has given of her time and talent to assist me in every way possible; thank you.

To Pastor Helen Pittman White, who spoke the Word of God over me and my family's life over twenty years ago, telling us what God would do.

To Lin Lombardi, PhD, who, in my opinion, is the consummate teacher and who has spent a lifetime shaping health-care policy while molding young minds. Dr. Lombardi serves as a mentor and friend who daily demonstrates the grace and wisdom under pressure in corporate America.

Introduction

A Standard of Confusion

Most corporations in America today profess and promote the corporate culture of human development in which all employees have a say in the operation and administration of the corporation. The disciplinary process is limited or replaced with training seminars, talent tree initiatives, coaching, and mentoring programs. The double standard of this culture is the very present subculture of all corporations that allows employees wide boundaries for politics, which lead to favoritism, cronyism, corruption, and the destruction of innocence and ethics.

The challenge for the Christian is in finding out how to navigate oneself through this corporate dynamic.

The corporate culture is a very noble one. What born-again saint would not want to be part of a system that helps develop the whole person, treats him or her with respect and dignity, and gives him or her a platform to express his or her creative side? The conflict arises when the same Christians who plan for righteousness find themselves surrounded by unrighteousness because biblical teachings instruct the believer not to have any fellowship with unbelievers.

> Do not be unequally yoked together with unbelievers for what fellowship has righteousness with lawlessness? And what communion has light with darkness.
> (2 Cor. 6:14)

So you see, being involved in coaching and mentoring as well as favoritism and cronyism, human development, and corruptive destruction is where corporate Christians must navigate their daily walk with Christ, trusting and believing that their daily walk is by faith and not by sight.

The doctrine of coaching is to instruct, train, teach, and tutor individuals or groups to enlighten their understanding and improve performance. In a corporate structure, this is viewed as human development, talent development, and/or employee development.

The doctrine of mentoring is to pair together or match up experienced, trusted advisors with their younger, inexperienced coworkers. This doctrine differs slightly from coaching since it is less forward and its scope of teaching is wider. It serves to teach more inexperienced employees the intangibles of corporate work life and how to and where to apply the lessons learned from coaching. It is the development of wisdom, which is the application of knowledge.

The doctrine of favoritism is the unfair favoritism of one person or group over another. Because of a lack of impartiality, this doctrine causes much division in any setting.

The doctrine of cronyism is the practice of hiring and/or promoting close friends and/or companions. This doctrine also causes much division in any setting.

The doctrine of corruption is the practice of bribery and fraud in any setting because of the moral deterioration of an individual or group.

Beloved, as you can see, the contrast between these doctrines are vast. Coaching and mentoring are noble doctrines worthy of being promoted because they promote care, concern, and compassion for one's fellow man and his ultimate betterment. Favoritism, cronyism, and corruption are certainly not noble doctrines. They are almost always practiced covertly because they promote the moral decay of the individual and/or corporation and the acceptable destruction of employees due to the stumbling blocks of partiality and division, which certainly hinder work performance and usher in deviant behavior.

Scripture teaches us that bad behavior always corrupts good morality. "Do not be deceived. Evil company corrupts good morality" (1 Cor. 15:33). When this process is accepted, the doctrine of the *normality of deviation* has been introduced to an already divisive environment, and corruption has taken hold. When bad morality goes unchecked and is allowed to operate, it becomes extremely difficult to stop. Like a slow-moving train, it will only pick up speed until it is derailed, and hopefully the collateral damage will not be too extensive.

Daniel 4:28-30

All this came upon King Nebuchadnezzar, at the end of the twelve months he was walking about the royal palace of Babylon. The king spoke, saying, "Is not this great Babylon, that I have built for a royal dwelling by my mighty power and for the honor of my majesty."

Chapter 1

The Promoted Corporate Culture

All this came upon King Nebuchadnezzar, at the end of the twelve months he was walking about the royal palace of Babylon. The king spoke, saying, "Is not this great Babylon, that I have built for a royal dwelling by my mighty power and for the honor of my majesty." (Dan. 4:28-30)

Beloved, it truly is a crying shame that what we love to promote is never the whole story but an edited version of our reality. King Nebuchadnezzar's opinion of his beloved Babylonian Empire was that it was the greatest royal dwelling place on earth, and it was built by his mighty power for his majesty. I'm sure the opinions of all the enslaved nations, victims of murdered loved ones, raped women and girls, and mutilated young boys who were affected by the Babylonian Empire would have been completely different.

Beloved, the Scriptures teach us that if you know the truth, that truth will make you free. What truth? It is the truth about us, who we are, and what we are capable of. Most corporations today have some kind of public relations department or firm promoting who they are and what they are, and this message is always seen from the eyes of the principals and very rarely from the staff.

But because of whom we are and what we bring to the corporation, two cultures co exist alongside each other, and they are the promoted culture and the hidden subculture. The promoted culture is the one the public sees and learns about but feels no effect from. The hidden subculture is never seen but often heard about, and the effects are seen and felt daily

Diversity

Diversity is a relatively new concept in the corporate environment. The modern-day doctrine of diversity finds it roots in the financial industry, specifically when dealing with investments and spreadsheets. The concept is to reduce the risk of loss of investments by investing in a wide variety of sectors.

In the corporate world, the concept has been changed from reducing to including. Every company in America today must legally operate as a racially, religiously, physically, and sexually blind entity and include all members of society. The problem with this new corporate transformed doctrine is that to truly be a racially, religiously, physically, and sexually blind business, one needs to document it, keep statistics on it, and label it to meet federal and local hiring standards. But at the same time, a truly diverse society that wants to be seen as a melting pot would not and should not divide its society or corporations with the terms of minority and majority because a corporation is a group of people authorized to act as one.

> There is neither Jew nor Greek, there is neither slave nor free, there is neither male nor female, for you are all one in Christ Jesus. (Gal. 3:28)

I have often wondered why this nation has such an insatiable appetite to label, compare, and compete one with others. Is it our history, DNA, culture, ego, and arrogance. I am not sure why, but I do know that this truly creates a massive subculture in our corporations, governments, and societies. This is especially true when you stop to think that our great republic was founded on the Latin doctrine of *E Pluribus Unum*, which, when broken down and translated from Latin, means this:

> *Pluribus* means plural. *Unum* means unit. *E Pluribus Unum* means many uniting into one, or as it was more accurately translated on our country's seal until 1956, "Out of Many One." This phrase was changed to "In God We Trust" in 1956.

Yet to date, true equality in the workplace is a distant dream. Because this dream is becoming such a reality, it has taken society's social problems and brought them right into corporate America. These problems create a subculture that promotes deviant standards of behavior. In the upcoming chapters, we will discuss more of this issue.

Human Development

> All scripture is given by inspiration of God and is profitable for doctrine, for reproof, for correction, for instruction in righteousness that the man of God may be complete thoroughly equipped for every good work. (2 Tim. 3:16)

Human development is based on the concept of developing the employee in the practical and philosophical issues of the corporation so said employee becomes a high-performing, socially encouraging, and good living representative of the corporation.

Training

Tools such as advanced, discipline-specific training, workplace violence training, sexual harassment training, diversity training, and a slew of others are used to accomplish this objective.

The problem with this concept, like any other legislation, is that it addresses the human intellectual system, which is influenced by the human ego system. It believes it's addressing the preverbal heart, but it's not. The human preverbal heart—better known as the soul—is the very seat of human thoughts, feelings, emotions, and motivations. Addressing anything else will lead to a complete failure to develop the individual.

"For the heart is deceitful above all things and desperately wicked, who can know it? "I the Lord search the heart. I test the mind, even to give every man according to his ways, according to the fruit of his doing." (Jer. 17:9-10)

Beloved, God is man's final judge, and He renders His judgment for man's works. Only by God are all actions weighed. Yet man still insists on behaving to a lesser standard that is grounded in emotions, selfishness and ego, which rivals the promoted culture.

Romans 7:19

For the good that I will to do, I do not; but the evil I will not to do, that I practice.

Chapter 2

The Unpromoted Subculture

In Romans 7:19, the apostle Paul describes the internal war that takes place inside of every single soul born of a woman. There is a struggle to live right, talk right, and think right. Scripture calls this right living or righteousness. As living souls in corporate America, we are striving daily to promote a noble corporate culture while practicing with consistent perfection the unpromoted subculture. These are things like the following:

> **Politics:** This is scheming or sly behavior or taking on or belonging to cliques during controversial matters. When politics enters the workplace, it always divides people, and division in a corporation is never a good

thing. A corporate body is designed to act as one, not many. Politics in the workplace are the first signs of something going wrong with the promoted culture. It gives birth to schemes and sly, untrustworthy behavior. It creates separation among staff members and forces them to work against one another for competing interests. The tools of this competition are gossip, lying, and slander.

Favoritism: This is unfairly favoring one person or group at the expense of another. This is a big byproduct of political activity in a corporate environment and reaps devastating problems for any corporation. It hinders productivity, kills morale, creates mistrust among staff and groups, and often begets violence. This ism should be avoided at all cost.

Cronyism: This is the hiring and/or promotion of friends and family. This ism tends to make the playing field very uneven. It dismisses the concept that hard work will always bring favorable rewards. Many parents practice this behavior in the workplace when they try to circumvent the hiring process to bring their children into the workforce. This problem is compounded when they bring their kids into high-level positions with little or no experience.

Corruption: This is the deterioration of morality and widespread corrupt practices. It is normally found in the purchasing or bidding process. Financial kickbacks for sales or contract services are wrong, but we find this behavior becoming very common at the executive levels of companies with corporate profit embellishment, value manipulation of stocks, insider trading, and so on.

These characteristics of a subculture can lead to *the destruction of ethics and innocence.* This creates the normalcy of deviation factor.

It causes problems in a corporation when people find that the main cultural standard is not working for them in their daily lives due to a subculture of politics, favoritism, cronyism, and corruption that deprives them of materialistic conveniences. They almost always deviate from that standard and create a deviant standard, which becomes their norm. This normalcy of deviation always starts with the destruction of ethics and innocence. The ethical boundaries become very blurred when deviant behavior is accepted as the norm

Sociologists see deviance as the result of a conflict between the culturally prescribed goals of society, such as material success, and the obstacles to obtaining them that some groups of people face.

The dynamics of this social and corporate problem can transform any good employee into a bad one. I would like to identify how the professing Christian employee should navigate through this maze. This is the point of this book, so let us look at the source of the believer's morality. Which is the foundation and center of their lives, everything else revolves around this center and is subjected to it.

II Corinthians 5:7

For we walk by Faith and not by sight.

Chapter 3

The Christian Faith

Beloved, you may have heard it said that the Holy Bible is made up of two testaments, old and new, which equals sixty-six books. Twenty-seven are in the New Testament and thirty-nine make up the Old Testament. Through all sixty-six books there is one message.

Panoptic Message of the Gospels

This is at the center of every believer's Christian character. Some describe this message by saying, "The New Testament is in the Old Testament concealed, and the Old Testament is in the New Testament revealed."

As human beings, we have been created and designed to be social beings, so relationships are a foundational part of our existence on the planet, whether they be working relationships, emotional relationships, sexual relationships, or business relationships. Whatever the relationship is, it should be managed based on the concept of service and that God is first, relationship second, and self last. Believers should put an emphasis on having a vertical relationship with God, which will always benefit the horizontal relationships. By their basic nature, man's relationships without God are always characterized by strife and contention, but with God they are characterized by peace and harmony.

Philosophy of the Gospel

Some may say this philosophy of life based on the gospel is a farce because more wars have been fought on the earth because of religion than any other reason, and I would wholeheartedly agree.

Religion introduces man to God, and relationships let man know God. There is a vast difference between knowing about God and knowing God. One can learn about God from third parties, a pastor, seminary schools, videos, and audio teaching tools, all of which are designed to grow faith. (Faith comes by hearing and hearing by the word of God [Rom. 10:8].) Faith comes by hearing the message about Christ.

But only when one meets Christ and develops a relationship with Him will one's psyche and character be so impacted that it transforms one's very human nature. Christians call this change or transformation sanctification or living free from the pull of the subculture.

During this process, our nature is overpowered by God's Spirit as He imparts His nature or the characteristics of His spirit into us. These are known as the fruits of the spirit or rewards of the spirit. They are love, joy, peace, longsuffering, kindness, goodness, faithfulness, gentleness, and self-control (Gal. 5:22).

Folks who know a little bit about God may display a form of these characteristics, but these godly attitudes characterize the lives of only those who belong to God by faith in Christ and who have spent time knowing Him and who possess His spirit. Now understand, this is where the rubber meets the road on how the corporate Christian should easily navigate the land mines of the corporate subculture and environment.

The Practicality of This Philosophy

The spirit of God produces fruits or rewards that consist of nine characteristics or attitudes that are inextricably linked with each other and commanded of believers throughout their lives. All can agree on these practical attitudes because they cause no strife or contention among men. The first fruit is love, not an emotional or physical attraction love but rather a respect, devotion, and affection *love* that leads people to be willing to give self-sacrificial service. *Joy* is not the result of favorable circumstances but occurs even when the circumstances are the most painful and severe. It's a happiness based on unchanging divine promises, a sense of well-being all the time. *Peace* is the inner calm that comes from the confidence in one's relationship with Christ. Like joy, peace, is not related to one's circumstances.

Longsuffering is patience and grace in action or the ability to endure emotional injuries inflicted by others along with a willingness to accept irritating or painful situations. *Kindness* is a tender concern for others reflected in a desire to treat others gently. *Goodness* means having moral and spiritual excellence, which is kindness in action. *Faithfulness* is loyalty and trustworthiness in all relationships. *Gentleness* is a meek, humble, and gentle attitude, with no desire for revenge or retribution. *Self-control* is the ability to restrain one's passions and appetites.

Biblical doctrine teaches the believer that anyone walking by the spirit of God who manifests His fruit/rewards needs no external laws to produce the attitude and behavior that pleases God and man.

The Purity of the Gospel

> God is love and he who abides in love abides in God and God in him. (1 John 4:11)

It is not my intention to turn this book into a biblical lesson, but because the Holy Writ is known as the Living Word, it's really the only book on earth that is qualified to speak to man's heart, motives, and emotions. Scripture tells the believer that first and foremost love is the greatest gift God has ever given mankind. Of all the gifts God has given to mankind, love is the greatest and will last the longest. After all other gifts fade and fail, love will endure to the very end. It's not only the greatest gift but also the most powerful.

The foundation of the gospel is built on love. God so loved the world that He gave His only begotten Son, that whosoever believes in Him should not perish but have everlasting life (John 3:16). It's also maintained by love, for the power and purity of love transforms the human heart and changes the stubborn mind. It's the greatest and most powerful gift because it gives the individual who walks in it the power and purity to to suffer long and still be kind, the strength to resist envy and jealousy, the capacity to resist rude and disrespectful behavior, and the power not to be self-centered and consumed with one's own feelings and needs. It does not respond to provoking and antagonistic offenses, turns from evil thinking, won't be happy in negativity, and will seek and rejoice in the truth.

This gift of love is action, not abstraction. Positive love will always be patient with people and gracious to them with generosity. It's devoted to truth in everything with regard to all things, and this godly love will always protect, believe, hope, and endure what others reject. So if the believer activates the central core of their faith developed morality which is a new philosophical view wrapped in a simple practical package and delivered with the utmost sincerity and purity they will be that unifying force who is able to stand strong in the face of the corporate sub-culture.

―――⋄⊙⋄―――

A Corporation is a group of people authorized to act as an individual and recognized in law as a single entity.

―――⋄⊙⋄―――

Chapter 4

A Corporation

The *Oxford American Dictionary* defines a corporation as, "A group of people authorized to act as an individual and recognized in law as a single entity, especially in business, no matter what that business industry is." Most corporate structures are a grouping of different positions and departments within a company, which all have separate tasks and assignments but work together to operate as one company. Many large companies tend to have similar corporate structures, which often include a marketing department, finance department, human resources department, and information technology department. The hierarchy of job positions within this structure includes a chief executive officer or president, board members, managers, and line staff, union and nonunion.

As you begin to put together all of these departments, assignments, position, and titles, and there is a hierarchy of order with individuals performing their very completely different tasks and trying to be the best they can be. It does not take long to see what happens. Now remember what we said: the normalcy of deviation is what happens when there is a conflict between the culturally prescribed goals of society or an entity (such as material, psychological, emotional success) and the obstacles to obtaining them that some groups of people face.

This typical prototype model of any corporation in the hands of fallen man is destined to have a rocky road on its way to achieving its corporate objective. Most corporations use their promoted culture, which is educational in nature, to facilitate and coordinate all of these different positions, departments, disciplines, and tasks. To keep each employee focused on the goals and objectives of the corporation as stated earlier, the educational tools used are meant to mature the work force and eliminate petty, immature behavior. Tools such as diversity training are also used to promote inclusion and combat exclusive attitudes.

Human development training such as conflict resolution, workplace violence, and verbal and nonverbal communication training are all designed to combat the natural differences and frictions that are created by the competitive environments corporations facilitate.

While the promoted culture is educating its workforce through a philosophical doctrine of oneness, the unpromoted subculture is creating a practical standard of performance to meet the material, psychological, and emotional success desired by individuals, groups, departments, and positions. Practical tools used are: politics, which is to exploit political relationships in an opportunistic, manipulative, and devious way; favoritism, which is to favor one group or person over another for career advancement; cronyism, which is to favor friends and/or family in matters of professional appointments; and corruption, which is moral perversion and disintegration of integrity in financial, professional, and emotional matters. These will certainly lead to the complete destruction of ethics and innocence and replace them with the normalcy of deviation, where it becomes very normal and comfortable to deviate from the highest standard of professional performance to the lowest one.

When this condition takes root in the human heart, only an act of God can remove it. The reason why this condition is so devastating to the corporation is because when people, no matter where they are in the corporate structure, bring to the table excitement and enthusiasm based on an expectation of a rewarding and fulfilling career, with a hope of making the theoretical become actual with the tools of the promoted culture. Then they are confronted with the unpromoted subculture and are totally unprepared. Hopes and dreams are destroyed, careers are altered, attitudes are changed, outlooks become angry, and the future becomes uncertain.

The unpromoted subculture develops in employees a total contamination of their hearts, which is the nature of man. A hurt heart or emotions, along with bruised egos, almost always lead to a natural distancing and shutting down of people's natures to the cause of their pain. This heart can easily turn into a cold, headstrong heart or nature. Along with the loss of solid moral guidance, this nature becomes stubborn and self-willed. Only God can fix this kind of brokenness because a headstrong heart is a stubborn, self-willed nature and a loss of spirit, and hope is the loss of right governance of one's mind.

In the book of Ezekiel, we find God performing this cleansing transformation on a national scale with

His people as He was about to bring them back out of figurative and literal captivity. Ezekiel 36:26 says, "I will give you a new heart and put a new spirit within you; I will take the heart of stone out of your flesh and give you a heart of flesh." The figurative and literal interpretation of this Scripture is the gift of the new heart signifies a new birth, which is regeneration by the Holy Spirit. The heart stands for the whole nature of a man, and the spirit is his governing power of the mind, which directs thought and conduct. A strong heart is stubborn and self-willed. A heart of flesh is pliable and responsive. The evil inclination is removed, and a new nature replaces it.

This insidious and infectious subculture kills the entire ethical and innocent operating system and must be completely wiped clean. Only God can clean the human computer. When people are trapped in a subculture mentality, they are there due to some kind of trauma that has caused a fracture in their life and work life perspective. This contrast of where they are and where they need to be in their perspective of their environment is vast and sometimes never bridged unless they hear the life resurrecting message of the gospel.

II Corinthians 4:8

We are hard-pressed on every side, yet not crushed. We are perplexed, but not in despair, persecuted, but not forsaken, struck down but not destroyed.

Chapter 5

The Continental Divide

> We are hard-pressed on every side, yet not crushed. We are perplexed, but not in despair, persecuted, but not forsaken, struck down but not destroyed. (2 Cor. 4:8)

The division between the gospel and the corporate message is vast in purposes, design, audience, benefit, and outcome.

The Motivation of the Message

Both messages have noble qualities and appeal to segments of the population, and both are viewed as dangerous and divisive. No reasonable-thinking person would ever argue against or reject concepts like love thy neighbor, turn the other cheek, help the poor, feed the hungry, clothe the naked, and protect the fatherless. Quite a few do reject the exclusivity of the gospel and that is salvation is a gift from God through faith in Jesus Christ alone. No man comes to the Father except through the Son Jesus alone. In today's society, this exclusivity is difficult to accept, even among the saints. By the same token, most reasonable-thinking folk are in complete agreement with conscious-minded corporations who accept responsibility for the environment, show fairness toward their employees, and consider people over profits. But most will not support corporate greed and corruption, unfair treatment of unions, and violations of collective bargaining gains. Where both messages differ is where the rubber meets the road.

To really see and understand the messages of the corporation as to the gospel is to look at their purpose, mission, and vision for themselves and the environment around them. All companies exist to do something and do that something well. Most measure how well they achieve their purpose, mission, and vision by financial realities. Even nonprofit companies with 501C(3) tax status try very hard not to lose money, even if they don't make any. Most companies exist first for themselves and their own purposes, meaning if its needs are not met first, there might not be a company. This doctrine of self runs counter to everything in relationship building. In any relationship, if one side only is getting its needs met, that relationship will not last long. One cannot be in a relationship by oneself with an expectation that others will stay around.

In Abraham Maslow's 1943 paper "A Theory of Human Motivation," Maslow studied what he called exemplary people—Albert Einstein, Jane Addams, Eleanor Roosevelt, and Frederick Douglas—and came up with the theory that all human beings have five basic needs that must be met at all times in their lives. They are the following:

- **Physiological needs**: These are the literal requirements for human survival, like air, food, water etc. If these needs are not met, the human body cannot function.
- **Safety needs:** When physical needs are satisfied, individuals' safety needs take precedence and dominate behavior. In the absence of physical safety due to terrorist attacks, war, natural disaster, or in cases of family violence or childhood abuse, these safety needs manifest themselves in such things as a preference for job security, grievance

procedures, savings accounts, and insurance policies. Safety and security needs include personal security, financial security, health, and well-being.

- **Love and belonging needs:** After the physiological and safety needs are fulfilled, next come the social needs of humans, which involve feelings of belonging. This can come from a large social group, such as clubs, offices, cultures, or religious groups.
- **Esteem Needs:** After the first three needs have been satisfied, esteem needs becomes increasingly important. These include the need for things that reflect on self-esteem, personal worth, social recognition, and accomplishment and how we want others to perceive us.
- **Self-Actualization Needs:** This is the highest level of Maslow's hierarchy of needs. Self-actualizing people are self-aware, concerned with personal growth, less concerned with the opinions of others, and are interested in fulfilling their potential. They are focused on trying to become everything they are capable of becoming.

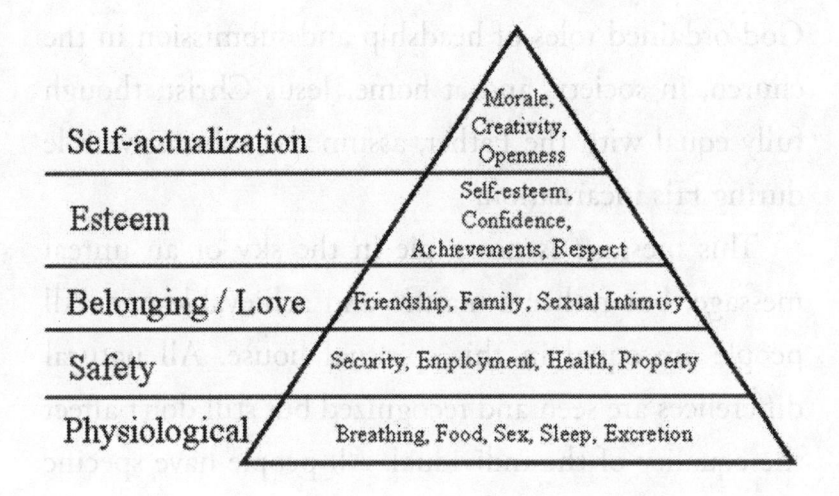

```
                    /\
                   /  \
                  /Morale,\
Self-actualization/Creativity,\
                /  Openness   \
               /----------------\
              / Self-esteem,     \
    Esteem   /  Confidence,       \
            / Achievements, Respect \
           /--------------------------\
Belonging / Love  Friendship, Family, Sexual Intimicy
         /------------------------------\
  Safety /  Security, Employment, Health, Property \
        /--------------------------------------------\
Physiological  Breathing, Food, Sex, Sleep, Excretion
      /------------------------------------------------\
```

This diagram represents Abraham Maslow's hierarchy of needs that drives his theory of human motivation

The Gospel Message

> There is neither slave nor free, there is neither male nor female, for you are all one in Christ Jesus. (Gal. 3:28)

This profound statement in the epistle of Paul to the Galatians says that all those who are one with Jesus Christ are also one with each other. It does not deny the racial, social, and sexual distinctions among Christians but does affirm that those do not imply spiritual inequality before God, nor is the spiritual equality incompatible with the

God-ordained roles of headship and submission in the church, in society, and at home. Jesus Christ, though fully equal with the Father, assumed a submissive role during His incarnation.

This message is not a pie in the sky or an unreal message, but rather a mature and achievable one. All people are equal in this spiritual house. All natural differences are seen and recognized but still don't affect the equality of the individual. All people have specific roles to fill and grow into, and all need each other to be successful.

As we get closer to the heart of the division between the gospel message and the corporate purpose, we find the difficult road that hundreds of thousands of corporate Christians live on a daily basis, some successful, most struggling, compromising, and suffering from a loss of control of their own feelings, hopes, and dreams.

The Believer versus the Employee

No one can serve two masters, for either he will hate one and love the other, or else he will be loyal to the one and despise the other. You cannot serve God and mammon. Matthew 6:24 Beloved, here is the complexity of the corporate Christian's journey. No human being can continuously serve two masters. No human being can continuously be torn between two lovers, no more than you can safely stand in the middle of a highway. You will be in danger of either side of traffic. In biblical times, as in present times, people believed devotion to money and devotion to God were perfectly compatible. It was confirmation of the belief that earthly riches signified divine blessings, so they believed that folks with money were therefore God's favorite folks.

The belief in a financial system that promotes money as an end all to all things, especially a good quality of life, drives the believer into the mind-set of the employee, and in this quagmire we find the complete doctrine of the corporate promoted and unpromoted cultures being merged into a perverted message of the gospel.

As long as I keep my job, salary, and position, it's because of the favor of God, no matter how ruthless my behavior has become. Why? Because devotion to money and God are one and the same. It takes great strength and discipline to extract oneself from such a quagmire and even more not to be lured into it. Now Jesus Christ Himself was also tempted by this systematic process. In Matthew 4, we find Christ in the wilderness about to start His earthly ministry, and He was attacked on three different fronts. The first one was designed to satisfy the physical body, the second one was designed to satisfy a proud heritage, and the third one was designed to satisfy visual lust for power.

Beloved, the believer must always remember that there are only three ways one can be tempted. Only three windows or portals are open for us to be seduced into compromising behavior. It started way back in the Garden of Eden when Satan introduced sin or rebellious behavior to Eve in Genesis 3:6: "So when the woman saw that the tree was good for food [lust of the flesh], that it was pleasant to the eyes [lust of the eyes] and a tree desirable to make one wise [pride of life]." If believers have any of these windows open in their lives, surely seduction will find it and sinful rebellious behavior will follow. Any employee of a company who finds himself or herself caught up in the unpromoted subculture has these window wide open, and the dangerous thing about this is that these feelings and emotions tend to feel good to the individual who is caught up in them and knows no better.

> But each one is tempted when he is drawn away by his own desire and enticed. Then when desire has conceived, it gives birth to sin and sin, when it is full-grown, brings forth death. (James 1:14-15)

The concept or pattern of temptation dangles enticements to lure our desires or hidden desires to the surface, and after the pleasure of conception of these desires, sin is born, but sin can't be trusted. Even though it's your sin, when it grows up, it will try to destroy you financially, occupationally, emotionally, psychologically, spiritually, and in some cases physically.

The Rewards and Benefits

> And you shall remember the Lord your God for it is He who gives you power to get wealth that he may establish His covenant which He swore to your fathers as it is this day. (Deut. 8:18)

Most Americans today don't find their jobs very rewarding. They don't make enough money, they work too many hours, the career advancement process is unfair, and they don't like their bosses. However, there are some real, tangible rewards and benefits we all enjoy but don't realize or participate in. Most will identify their rewards as a paycheck and benefits, such as health and life insurance, but Scripture teaches us that God has something bigger in mind. He says, "I give you power to get wealth." Your paycheck is not given to you. You really do earn it. Your power is displayed in your endurance to get up every morning and go get it in spite of how you feel—in spite of your letdowns and disappointments. This power is not yours but is given to you from an endless supply source. It's been given to you for a very specific reason. The concept here is stewardship, not ownership.

The reason for this power and wealth is to establish and present an open invitation to this rewarding covenant relationship agreement between God and you. Another reward and benefit is worry- and stress-free living because of this power. The purpose and covenant are God's. He's responsible for the planning and implementation; all you have to do is be faithful and show up. Another reward and benefit is the gratifying feelings that come from being obedient to God's Word and commandments, which produces and manifests Christian compassion in your daily life. Other rewards and benefits that come from the gospel message and the corporate culture are some very close lifelong friendships and the opportunity to help, support, and achieve goals together, share in great rewards, and learn from terrible mistakes. The most important one for the Corporate Christian is the soul-satisfying work and endless opportunity to share your faith and make someone's day a little brighter and emotions a little lighter. This new found purpose is very consuming and brings about a complete change of attitude and motivation that drives the believer to seek co-existence rather then separation.

II Corinthians 5:17

Therefore if anyone is in Christ he is a new creation old things have passed away behold all things have become new.

Chapter 6

The Coexistence

Therefore if anyone is in Christ he is a new creation old things have passed away behold all things have become new. Now all things are of God, who has reconciled us to Himself through Jesus Christ and has given us the ministry of reconciliation. That is, that God was in Christ reconciling the world to Himself, not imputing their trespasses to them and has committed to us the word of reconciliation. Now then we are ambassadors for Christ as though God were pleading through us. We implore you on Christ's behalf be reconciled to God. For He made Him who knew no sin to be sin for us, that we might become the righteousness of God in Him. (2 Cor. 5:17-21)

Beloved, this is the foundation of our salvation to spread the good news to all who have an ear to hear. The Scripture is saying that God Himself through Christ reconciled us back to Himself. He brought us into agreement with Him and made us consistently compatible with Him, *in perfect harmony.* The born-again believer takes on the responsibility of the office of the minister of reconciliation to win hostile people to friendliness and become amicable to God and the gospel message.

The Covenant

The Bible has eight covenants, which fall into two classes: conditional and unconditional. We live in the dispensation of the last one, known as the New Testament. It is a new covenant with Israel in contrast with the Old Testament. Christ Jesus, by His blood, is the mediator of this new covenant, which was inaugurated at the cross and is described in Scripture as "enacted or better promises" (Heb. 8:6). The mediator of this covenant has become, for all mankind, "the source of eternal salvation" (Heb. 5:9) to all who obey Him, as well as the cornerstone and head of the church (Eph. 2:20-22), which is being built during this dispensation. The individuals who are being called out are both Jews and Gentiles alike. Ultimately and literally, this new covenant, with its unconditional and external blessings, will be established with Israel at Christ's second advent to earth.

This covenant promises eternal life after the grave and not eternal damnation. It's an unconditional promise of salvation if one confesses with one's mouth the Lord Jesus and believes in one's heart that God raised Him from the dead. This process is called the three Ps. The first one is being saved from the *penalty* of sin, or salvation, the second one is being saved from the *pull* of sin, or sanctification, and third one is being saved from the *presence* of sin, or glorification. Based on this process, the motivation for the reconciliation work is developed in the believer.

The Responsibilities of Both

I say, then, walk in the spirit and you will not fulfill the lust of the flesh, for the flesh lusts against the spirit and the spirit against the flesh, and these are contrary to one another so that you do not do the things that you wish. Gal 5: 16-17 Both the corporate Christian and the corporate employee have nonnegotiable responsibilities that must be fulfilled daily. If both parties stay true to their responsibilities, the work environment will be a much better place. The Christian must every day live after the spirit and not the flesh. All believers have the presence of the indwelling Holy Spirit as their personal power for living to please God. This is a continuous state or habitual lifestyle. This lifestyle is lived counter to the lifestyle of the flesh, which is the body, mind, will, and emotions, all of which are subject to sin. They represent man in his most unredeemed humanness. The flesh opposes the work of the spirit and will always try to lead the Christian toward sinful behavior.

The corporate employee has a responsibility to live according to the promoted corporate culture. Employees should always seek diversity or inclusiveness, strive for personal human development to reach their maximum potential, and be eager to be trained in new things and/or techniques. Unlike the Christian, the employee must depend on his or her own ethics and work standard to resist the pull of the corporate subculture that seeks to pull the employee away from the promoted culture and into a downward spiral of subpar work habits and a toxic work environment. So if both set of employees, the believer and nonbeliever, overcome their internal struggles, they are much better together than apart, and the company is far better off.

Stewardship or Ownership

> For the Kingdom of heaven is like a man traveling to a far country, who calls his own servants and delivered his goods to them, and to one he gave five talents, to another two and to another one to each according to his own ability, and immediately he went on a journey. (Matt. 25:14-15)

This wonderful parable represents the tragedy of wasted opportunity. The man who goes on a journey represents Christ, and the servants are professing believers who are given different levels of responsibility. Faithfulness is what he demands of them. If one reads the whole parable Matthew 25:14-30, it shows that faithfulness will always lead to fruitfulness in some degree. All employees of a corporation have a legal responsibility to be faithful and fruitful at their place of business, no matter where they are in the corporate structure. Some may say, "Of course they must be faithful, because the corporation pays their salary, pays their mortgage, funds their vacations, and supports their lascivious lifestyle." However, beloved, it goes a lot deeper than that. (Leaving it at a mere civil financial contractual agreement is to oversimplify the matter, like suggesting that rape happens because men are sexually aroused.)

This type of stewardship is based on servitude as one who is hired to manage another's property or resources. We must be good managers over this power source because we are not the owners or creators of it and have no legal right to abuse or misuse it, because tapping into one's soul—the seat of human motivations, feelings, and emotions—and pulling out the blueprint to maximize potential has nothing to do with compensation packages.

All men and women, saints and sinners alike, have in them the potential to be great. Why are some successful and others not? Now as I explain this, let us not put any Hollywood definitions of what greatness is and just say that all people who have the ability and self-awareness to maximize their moments and reach their true potential in any endeavor have achieved greatness. Any corporation has a right to demand faithfulness from its workforce as its workforce has the right for the corporation to be faithful to them. This means that all employees should at any given time perform to the very best of their abilities in spite of the environment they find themselves in. Faithfulness is a state of being and not a product of an environment.

Whether an employee is in the promoted culture or unpromoted subculture, faithfulness is expected because faithfulness will always lead to some degree of fruitfulness. This is being a good steward of something bigger then one's feelings, emotions, and behavior. Employees who purpose in their hearts to receive a compensation package but only perform on a conditional basis depending on how they feel because they just got promoted or disciplined is an employee who is practicing the highest form of hypocrisy, for the faithfulness and commitment is to himself or herself and not the corporation as a whole. This is being an owner of one's needs and nobody else's. This is where the believer can help these types of employees with their own reconciling behavior process, so that it lines up with their companies expectations of them.

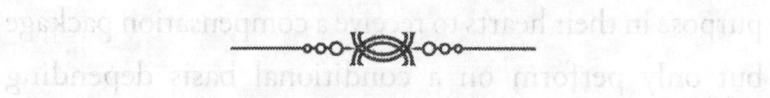

Exodus 2:11-12

Now it came to pass in those days, when Moses was grown that he went out to his brethren and looked at their burdens and he saw an Egyptian beating a Hebrew, one of his brethren. So he looked this way and that way and when he saw no one, he killed the Egyptian and hid him in the sand.

Chapter 7

Reconciliation of Christianity and Corporate Christians

Most corporate Christians find it very hard to express their faith in the corporate environment and in some cases their occupation in Christian settings. This conflict between belief and behavior can lead to a very lonely Christian journey because the gospel was designed to be shared by Christians and we were designed as social beings. If we fail to do this, a very big part of their lives are unfulfilled.

Scripture teaches us that *the Word of God* was authored, motivated, and inspired by the Holy Spirit, for prophecy never came by the will of man, but holy men of God spoke as they were moved by the Holy Ghost (2

Pet. 1:21). Scripture is not of human origin, nor is it the result of human will. No part of Scripture came about because man wanted it to be. Scripture also teaches us that there are diversities of gifts but the same spirit, and there are differences of ministries/administration but the same Lord. There are diversities of activities, but it is the same God who works all in all. The manifestation of the spirit is the same to each one for the profit of all, for to one is given the word of wisdom through the spirit to another the word of knowledge through the same spirit to another faith by the same spirit, to another gifts of healings by the same spirit (1 Cor. 12:4-9).

The Spirit of God

Corporate Christian executives—no matter what industry they find themselves in: legal, criminal justice, health care, education, financial, entertainment, sports, manufacturing, sales, marketing, etc.—must first know and believe these things about themselves. Your faith comes by hearing and hearing the Word of God. As God speaks to you through His Word, your faith increases.

The Holy Spirit authors and inspires His Word onto your heart, which increases your faith, boosts your confidence, and ignites your will, determination, and behaviors. Your unique gifts were given to you by the

Holy Spirit and can never be taken away from you by man. They will always make room for you, open doors for you, and close doors for you. You will always be assigned to someone or some place for a season or the rest of your life. "Then the spirit said unto Philip, go near and join thyself to this chariot" (Acts 8:29). The Holy Spirit knows where you'll be most effective, the very place where you gifts will flourish. Too many times we leave jobs for more money or because we don't like our bosses, and we never consult with the spirit of God. Then we learn that the grass it not always greener on the other side.

The Corporate Christian's Walk

So instead of running away from adversity, all Christian believers must first recognize and understand that their very first responsibility is to their God who called them. First, to be holy, faithful, and ministers of reconciliation, they must know and believe that what they have in them doesn't make them better. We're not called to be elitist. However, it will make you different, and your difference will make the corporation better. It will make your marriage better and your friendships better.

Your difference is the key to your success. Similarity breeds comfort, but differences create new ideas, break through old habits, and remove stumbling blocks. Anger is the spark that ignites your differences and births change in you. What gets you angry—laziness, gossip, politics, and favoritism? Moses got angry and delivered his people; Rosa Parks got angry and ignited the Civil Rights Movement. Your anger should always birth some kind of change in your life.

Once you start to deny this spiritual DNA from manifesting its behavior through you, you invite depression, bitterness, and resentment into your heart, and this kind of heart or nature can only find temporary satisfaction in the unpromoted subculture of any corporation. Reconciling the believer's call to his or her corporation is a win-win activity for all involved. Failure to complete this reconciliation put us outside the will of God for our lives, our success, our joy, and our happiness.

Reasons Why Reconciliation Is Never Done

There are many reasons why Christian executives don't reconcile their call and corporate responsibilities into one job and let go of all of the pressures of compromising their beliefs, values, and skills on their jobs or in their churches.

The first reason is lack of faith. Most believers forget that faith is an action and not abstraction. You must really work it for it to work for you. Faith never works because you hope or wish it will but because our faith in God is a Sunday-morning faith. We have not because we ask not, and when we ask we ask amiss *and* only to maintain the pleasure of an illusion. What is happening here, beloved, is that we have compromised our very call. This me-first generation seeks to enjoy and appropriate all of the benefits of being a Christian while taking on none of the burdens and obligations of that title. Put another way, we want a kind of Christianity that will serve our own self-centered aims and comfortably fit within the world we seek to create for ourselves. It is a help-me kind of help-me sainthood, "Lord, help me to achieve this! Lord, help me to acquire this! Lord, help me to attain this! Lord, help me to find this man, this woman!"

Beloved, this is how the system of miracles works. Tears don't move God, desperation does not intimidate God, manipulation does not control God, and education does not influence God; faith is the only voice God respects. Faith is the only method that impresses God to activate miracles. You must ask in faith.

God's two most important qualities as they relate to our lives are these:

- His only pain is our doubt of Him.
- His only pleasure is our belief in Him.

The second reason is fear.

> For God has not given us a spirit of fear, but of Power, and of love and of sound mind. (2 Tim. 1:7)

This is not a terrified, paralyzing fear but rather a cowardly, shameful fear that is caused by a weak, selfish character or nature. This self-centered, self-seeking, self-absorbed believer is more worried about man and his blessing than the Creator and blessings distributor.

Let's examine this kind of fear in the 2 Timothy. We find the apostle facing the escalating threats of

Roman persecution, resentful and hostile behavior from the people in the Ephesians church where he pastored who resented his leadership, and false teachers with sophisticated systems of deception. All of this may have been very overwhelming for him.

The corporate Christian executive today may face escalating persecution from someone who may be as powerful as Rome, along with colleagues who resent his or her position or promotion and the never-ending gossipers who sophisticatedly and deceptively spread untruths about him or her.

But like Timothy, if you become fearful, it did not come from God. He only gives us more power in times of trouble.

> But when they deliver you up, do not worry about how or what you should speak. For it will be given to you in that hour what you should speak, for it is not you who speak, but the spirit of your Father who speaks in you. God has already given us every spiritual resource needed for every trial and threat. All divine power that manifests effective, productive spiritual energy belongs to believers. (Matt. 10:19-20)

So when one chooses fear and weakness over faith and power, one is choosing selfishly, and with any good choice, there are always consequences to pay. These consequences may come in the form of the never ending pressures of feeling the need to justify and defend ones self, position and value to the company. This kind of pressure reek's havoc on our psychological and physical states and opens the door to stress factors.

Philippians 4:6-7

Be anxious for nothing, but in everything by prayer and supplication, with thanksgiving, let your request be made known to God; and the peace of God, which surpasses all understanding will guard your hearts, and minds through Christ Jesus.

Chapter 8
Stress Factors

> Be anxious for nothing, but in everything by prayer and supplication, with thanksgiving, let your request be made known to God; and the peace of God, which surpasses all understanding will guard your hearts, and minds through Christ Jesus. (Phil. 4:6-7)

In today's high-tech and fast-paced society, stress is a constant in the corporate environment. It is a real fact of our corporate environment that stress is related to both external and internal factors of our physical environment, including our jobs, relationships, homes, and all the other situation, challenges, difficulties, and expectations we are confronted with on a daily basis.

Our internal factors determine our bodies' ability to respond to and deal with external stress-inducing factors. The physical areas of the body affected most by stress are the brain and nervous system, muscles and joints, heart, stomach, pancreas, intestines, and reproductive system.

The most common somatic signs and symptoms that are brought on by stress are: sleep disturbances, muscle aches, gastrointestinal disturbances, and fatigue. Stress can also cause emotional and behavioral symptoms that include nervousness, anxiety, change in eating habits, including overeating, loss of enthusiasm, or energy and mood changes, like irritability and depression. People under stress show a greater tendency to engage in unhealthy behavior, such as excessive use of alcohol, drugs, and cigarettes.

The Foundation of Stress

Stress is how the internal man deals with the external pressure of life. In the Scripture from Philippians at the beginning of this chapter, we see the Lord giving us a wonderful antidote to the anxieties of life. When external pressures threaten the things in our lives that we have deep affections for, the ability to defend and/or deal with said forces creates internal stress on our bodies physically and emotionally. When the believer learns the secret of how to be anxious for nothing, he or she will create an internally stress-free environment for his or her life.

Fretting and worrying indicate a lack of trust in God's wisdom, sovereignty, and power and cultivates an attitude of trusting no one and trying to deal with all of life's problems by oneself. This is the typical approach of most believers and all nonbelievers in Christ. Due to a lack of trust, these individuals try a variety of avenues to deal with and/or overcome said external pressures.

- **Money:** Some folk trust that their net wealth can help them buy or create avenues out of these pressures.
- **Contacts:** Other folks believe that their contacts in high places can help lift them over the pressures of life.
- **Sympathy:** Others will play on a sympathetic ear to shield them from external pressures of corporate life—sympathies such as race, gender, age, living conditions, and/or unfair treatment.

But beloved, none of these avenues can adequately and successfully help to ease the burdens of stress in corporate life. This battle is fought on the inside of an individual in the heart of the mind—that place we call the soul where feelings, thoughts, and actions reside in the human being at the emotional part of human nature at the seat of feelings and sentiment. Only the Word of God, which is sharper than any two-edged sword, which can cut through the bone into the marrow, the deepest part of the human body, can get into the soul, the deepest part of the spiritual body and revive, rejuvenate, calm, and keep it from this anxiousness.

I Corinthians 12:12

For as the body is one and has many members, but all the members of that one body, being many, are one body, so also is Christ.

Chapter 9

Dysfunctional Behavior

> For as the body is one and has many members, but all the members of that one body, being many, are one body, so also is Christ. (1 Cor. 12:12)

The human body is one body with many members, all acting in concert together to move the body as one, and this is the desire of all corporate structures—that all members operate perfectly within their function.

Abnormal Behavior

In the human body, when a member begins to function differently from what it is designed to do, it is now displaying abnormal behaviors. It's not performing normally. As an organ or structure of the body, it's malfunctioning. In the summer of 2011, the United States witnessed the most dysfunctional congress in recent history, and because of its dysfunctional behavior, the main purpose for its creation was threatening the ability to govern. Because of this abnormal behavior, the country suffered a downgrade in its credit rating, the stock markets went into turmoil, and the nation suffered a reputation setback globally. Also, when corporate cultures are allowed to operate in a dysfunctional manner, they run the risk of failing to deliver on the main principle they were created to do. When this happens, said corporation is now malfunctioning, and any organization operating in an abnormal state will produce abnormal and subpar services and goods.

Psychological Reasons

Let us look one more time at the 2011 US Congress. The primary responsibility of politics and government is to affect people lives without them knowing you were even there. This should be done in the most-civilized societies through public infrastructures of safe, clean, and reliable public transportation systems; efficient and effective public educational systems that regenerate, evolve, and involve the character and nature of the innocent children; respectful and reliable civil servants;

impartial judicial systems; and a compassionate health care system. It also needs a well-run municipality that is not hindered by the fallen nature of man. If this is the normal standard of democratic governments, then how did we get to the spectacle of the summer of 2011?

There is a wonderful parable in Matthew 13:1-10 that talks about soil. It says:

> Behold, a sower went out to sow, and as he sowed, some seed fell by the wayside and the birds came and devoured them. Some fell on stony places, where they did not have much earth, and immediately sprang up because they had no depth of earth. But when the sun was up they were scorched and because they had no roots they withered away. And some fell among the thorns and the thorns sprang up and choked them. But others fell on good ground and yielded a crop: some a hundredfold, some sixty, some thirty.

Now beloved, understand that the work of governmental public service is a noble and honorable profession. So how does one answer this call and then become very corrupt and dishonorable in one's thoughts and deeds? Jesus explained the parable like this: Anyone who hears the word or call of the kingdom and does not understand it, the wicked one comes and snatches away what was sown in his or her heart, and this is those who received seed by the wayside. Anyone who receives seed on stony places and receives the word or call with joy but as soon as tribulation and persecution arise because of the word or call, they quickly stumble. Those who receive seed among the thorns are those who hear the word or call but the cares of this world and the deceitfulness of riches choke the word, and they become unfruitful. But he who received seed on good ground is he who hears the word or call and understands it and indeed bears fruit.

When people enter into public service without understanding the goal of public service in their minds and hearts, they pervert the foundation of public service from stewardship to ownership and from serving the masses who are the public to being served by the masses. This twisted manipulation of the process breeds a dangerous ideology of self-entitlement and fails to understand the paradox of the gospel and service.

The paradox is: the way down is the way up; that to be low is to be high; that the broken heart is the healed heart; that the contrite spirit is the rejoicing spirit; that the repenting soul is the victorious soul; that to have nothing is to possess everything; that to bear the cross is to wear the crown; that to give is to receive; and only in your darkness will you find His light, His joy in you sorrow, His grace in your sin, His riches in your poverty, His glory in your valley, and His life in your death.

This ideology of self is not about the collective but is only concerned with self-interest and begins to operate abnormally in the body. The reasons why this behavior is so dangerous is because it first distracts the group from its primary objective or main reason for existence, secondly it turns all attention and focus of the group inwardly so there is no self awareness or perception of where they are in relation to their objective and how they are being perceived by others, thirdly the group starts to battle amongst itself, a battle for dominion and dominance becomes the main focus and primary objective. At the end of this process no matter what transformation has taken place a sub-culture has been born and is extremely difficult to abort.

I Corinthians 14:33
For God is not the author of confusion but of peace as in all the churches of the saints.

Chapter 10

Disunity

For God is not the author of confusion but of peace as in all the churches of the saints. (1 Cor. 14:33)

Dissenting Behavior

Beloved, the key ingredient to disunity is certainly dissenting behavior from agreed-upon norms. Dysfunctional and abnormal behavior by certain members of an organization create great dissension among the group. Beloved, the problem with disunity is what it prevents among people and organizations. God's principle of unity is so powerful that an arrogant and perverted mankind was seeking to build the tower of Babel—a city whose top would be in heaven. God said, "Indeed the people are one and they all have one language, and this is what they begin to do, now nothing that they propose to do will be withheld from them" (Gen. 11:6).

Reasons for Dissenting Behavior

When people join a group and swear to operate according to the rules, regulations, and by-laws of that group or organization but increasingly demonstrate disunity or dissenting behavior, clearly something is going on in the individuals' hearts and reconciling the group's or organization's rules and regulations with their cultural background and belief system. Now understand that dissenting behavior is a very healthy thing, but causing division and discord among a group is a totally different thing. As a matter of fact, of all the Scriptures in the Bible, this is one of the six that God hates. It's even an abomination to Him (Prov. 6:16-19). These six things the Lord hates, yes, seven are an abomination to Him. A proud look, a lying tongue, hands that shed innocent blood, a heart that devises wicked plans, feet that are swift in running to evil, a false witness who speaks lies, and one who sows discord among brethren.

One who is operating in a divisive manner with an intention to divide is operating in more than cultural differences but something more dangerous. In most circumstances, the root cause of this can be found in the ego system, which perpetuates an insatiable appetite to be right no matter the cost. This childish and immature behavior can be seen displayed in board rooms, committee meetings, sports teams, professional and nonprofessional groups, not-for-profit organizations, churches, and even military institutions. When this attitude is on display, we truly miss out on great accomplishments.

God's Principle of Unity

This principle of unity is so powerful that in order for God to prevent humanity from accomplishing its vision for the tower, He had to divide them. When people are united, they can accomplish anything. The walls of Jericho can fall, empires will be defeated, armies can be turned to flight, men can walk on the moon, and the sick can be healed, the hungry fed, and the naked clothed.

Now, beloved, to understand this principle, let's take a closer look at the Genesis 11 story. Before we can understand why an almighty God would destroy a united society and cause chaos on the earth, we must take a biblical look through the Scriptures to get a clearer picture of the events. A biblical patriarch named Noah had three sons, Shem, Ham, and Japheth. After the biblical flood, these sons had sons of their own, but for the sake of expediency, let us focus on the middle son, Ham, who had six sons. One of those six sons was named Nimrod, a mighty hunter and warrior before God. Nimrod created several cities in the land of Shinar, which was ancient Mesopotamia and then Babylon and now is Iraq. In this land, Nimrod founded Babel, Erech, Accad, and Calneh, all of which are in modern-day Iraq.

Noah's family was given instructions by God not to only repopulate the earth but also to continue the work of Adam and Eve in Genesis 1:28: "Be fruitful and multiply fill the earth and subdue it have dominion over the fish of the sea, over the birds of the air and over every living thing that moves on the earth." God gave Noah the same instructions in the same region as the Garden of Eden in Genesis 9:1, "So God blessed Noah and his sons, and said to them: be fruitful and multiply and fill the earth, and the fear of you and the dread of you shall be on every beast of the earth and on all the fish of the sea. They are given into your hands."

So as Noah and his family went out with this great, awesome assignment, because man was made in the image of God, the gift of language was given to him so man and God could speak to each other while the work was done in unity with God and man. There is something very powerful about one nation that's focused on single-minded purpose for the betterment of all. Japan was able to create this type of unity after near annihilation by two atomic bombs to have the premier automobile companies in the world in Nissan and Honda and another premier company in Seiko watches. Nimrod and his nations decided to use the gift of language to abandon their God-ordained work for the apostate worship of self and pride at Babel. They were so united to do all their hearts desired to do that God had to come down and scatter the people by dividing them by language. Unity is a powerful principle when used for the greater good of the whole collective.

This is the primary problem with our churches today is a lack of unity. The answer to the question that Tavis Smiley proposed a few years ago, "What's wrong with the black church?" is a lack of unity. Whether it be because of race, finances, cultures, or geographical considerations, it all violates the request that our Lord Jesus prayed to His Father for in John 17:11: "Now I am no longer in the world, but these are in the world, and I come to you. Holy Father keep through your name those whom you have given me, that they may be one as we are." In unity there is peace, productivity, and joy, but in disunity, there is dissension, chaos, disagreements, and unhappiness. The body of Christ represents a diverse group of human beings living as a homogenous family in thought, belief and behavior. We are all the same in the spirit and soul.

In our society today, all of our most-successful sports teams operate in the uniqueness of sameness and oneness. They have the ability to always put a great product on the field or court.

I Corinthians 14:40

Let all things be done decently and in order.

Chapter 11

Disorderly Conduct

Let all things be done decently and in order. (1 Cor. 14:40)

Decency and Order

Every society and organization alike must have order to survive; order is a part of life. All corporations operate in their own order, which is found in their bylaws and mission statements. These are supported and enforced by their policies and procedures. All of these are designed for the corporation to operate successfully for what it was created to do. Another characteristic that should always be present with order is decency. All things in society as well as in corporations must always act decently and in order.

Many disputes and misunderstandings are resolved through decent behavior. But in most circumstances where there is no decency, you'll find very little order. Most strikes and class-action lawsuits are based on indecent behavior that violates or offends the individual's sense of worth before it violates any collective bargaining agreements. It is not decent to lay off workers and cap or suspend raises while corporate profits are prospering. It is not decent behavior to practice corruption, favoritism, and/or cronyism for the benefit of a few while rigorously enforcing the same rules to prevent it on others. It is not decent behavior to tolerate any type of discrimination or sexually offensive behavior at any level in an organization. Beloved, I believe based on the promise of reasonableness that reasonable people have a lot of common ground to resolve all types of differences and the ability to identify the behaviors that reasonably offend and create conflict.

Responsibility for Order

Beloved, this burden of obligation is upon all of us. We are all responsible to make sure decency and order are the primary things in our organizations. Abdication of this responsibility led to the Penn State University scandal, the Catholic church's reprehensible behavior, and the Enron and WorldCom shenanigans, along with the hundreds of class-action lawsuits that litter the highways of time in our nation just because a few folks could not act decently and in order.

Diffusion of Responsibility

This is then perpetuated by a diffusion of group responsibility where the responsibility for an outcome is diffused or spread among many people, reducing each individual's personal sense of accountability. This diffusion of responsibility almost always runs counter to the gospels' standards of personal morality.

Now you may think I am simplifying complex issues of governance and corporate doctrine, and you may be right in some small way, but beloved, in all situations and circumstances man is involved in—and when I say man, I'm not just talking about the gender but rather the species, because women don't always act right as well—no matter what circumstances humans find themselves in, they have a choice about how they will behave in thought and deeds. In Christendom, the church must decide whether it will pursue evangelism over economics while the corporation must decide whether it will put its people over its profits. I believe in both cases, it is a very easy decision because the right kind of evangelism as the right kind of employee will always lead to increase not only economically but also in fulfillment, human development, corporate efficiency, and a good name.

Revelation 7:13-14

Then one of the Elders answered, saying to me, "Who are these arrayed in white robes, and where did they come from?" and I said to him, "Sir you know," so he said to me, "These are the ones who come out of the great tribulation, and washed their robes and made them white in the blood of the lamb."

Chapter 12

Rising Out of the Ashes, a Bright Future

Then one of the Elders answered, saying to me, "Who are these arrayed in white robes, and where did they come from?" and I said to him, "Sir you know," so he said to me, "These are the ones who come out of the great tribulation, and washed their robes and made them white in the blood of the lamb." (Rev. 7:13-14)

This Scripture in the book of Revelation depicts a scene from the apostle John's vision of life on earth after the church has been taken out of the earth. Its theme is about how unparalleled judgment is always accompanied by unparalleled grace in salvation.

Now That We're Here

As our nation and world struggle with the worst economic crisis in the history of mankind, every aspect of life will be affected: every race of people, every society and culture, and every industry. As all of us deal with these financial uncertainties that can adversely affect our way of life, individually and collectively, let's always remember that there will be only one solution for our society as well as our organizations. No individual aspect of life or society can be targeted as the blame or solution, so now is not the time for panic or finger pointing but rather for some deep soul searching for each of us on how we can improve our fellow coworkers' lot during these difficult times.

Most corporations and municipalities respond pretty much the same way to fiscal uncertainties. They withdraw. They cut back on spending, which usually means they cut jobs. Some do it through attrition while others do it through layoffs and head counts, but in most cases, this kneejerk reaction is not always the best way because it carries with it long-term ramifications for the employee's and employer's relationship. Layoffs and downsizing hurt morale and create trust issues between those being laid off and those doing the laying off. While it saves money, a better model that is used by the Japanese car company Toyota is called lean or A3 thinking, which is designed to reduce waste and make a workforce lean and fit by using every available resource at its deposal before hiring more resources or letting go any resources.

A Legacy of Integrity

As we go through the muddy waters of uncertainty and deal with all of the antics of the organizational subculture from the board room to the break room, we as believers in Christ must always remember that we are called to be transformational and not conform to standards beneath the high calling of God, as difficult as this process can be. Our integrity and adherence to Christ's high standard of living are worth so much more then fleeting silver and gold. Dr. Martin Luther King Jr. once said that the true test of a man's character is not where he stands in times of comfort and convenience but rather where he stands during times of chaos and conflict.

Beloved, I believe Moses knew something about this kind of standing. When you find yourself feeling like you're standing alone and you can't find anybody willing or able to stand with you, just follow Moses's example and stand on the promises of our God, for he who dwells in the secret place of the Most High will abide under the shadow of the Almighty. God will be your refuge and fortress, and in Him you will trust. Why? Because He promised this:

> Because He has set His love upon me. Therefore I will deliver him; I will set him on high, because he has known my name. He shall call upon me, and I will answer him; I will be with him in trouble; I will deliver him and honor him, with long life I will satisfy him and show him my salvation. (Ps. 91:14-16)

This is His promise and pledge to us if we will just trust Him, believe Him, and receive Him.

The Power of Difference

What the corporate Christian must first understand is that God called us to be different at all times in all situations. We have had our souls, psyches, and thought processes impacted and affected by the God of Abraham, Isaac, Jacob, space, interstellar space, and the cosmos. This does not make us better but must make us different.

We are not supposed to respond to the stress, pressure, and pain of corporate subcultures like everyone else, for each of us has been called first to be faithful and then transformational. We don't follow public opinion, but rather we shape it by our character, behavior, and presence so we may help everyone see a better and new perspective to the same old tricks and schemes of our enemy. In Isaiah 59:19, the Holy Writ says this about the corporate Christian:

> So shall they fear the name of the Lord from the west and his glory from the rising of the sun; when the enemy comes in like a flood, the spirit of God will lift up a standard against him.

Who is the standard? We are this high standard and are called to lift people out of the floods of stinking thinking that can saturate the mind and control the soul.

So in conclusion, allow me to remind you that we are the architects and builders of our current and future corporations. If we are willing to draft a new plan for ourselves and start some internal construction, that can bridge belief and behavior so they can be synonymous with one another so when people see or talk about us, we can show and offer a blueprint of how beliefs can coexist and agree with or complement behavior. Our yeas should always be yeas, and our nays always nay. This is the cautious, circumspect walk that believers are called to walk every day of their lives. It provides them with a wonderful antidote to the corporate subculture. "See then that you walk circumspectly, not as fools but as wise, redeeming the time because the days are evil" (Eph. 5:15).

Endnote

- Stanley Eitzen, Author, Shirley Davis, Editor, Social Problems Second Edition (Allyn and Bacon Inc. 1980)
- John Mac Arthur, Author, John Mac Arthur, Editor, The Mac Arthur Study Bible (Word Publishing 1997)
- Abraham Maslow, Author, A. Theory of Human Motivation (Paper 1943)
- Dana Carson, Author, One True King (Dana Carson Ministries 2010)
- John MacArthur, Author, Hard To Believe (Nelson Books 2003)
- Mike Murdock, Author The Law of Recognition(Wisdom International 2007)

NOTES

NOTES

NOTES

NOTES